SPOTLIGHT ON NATIONS

INDIA

LORI DITTMER

CREATIVE EDUCATION · CREATIVE PAPERBACKS

Published by Creative Education and Creative Paperbacks
P.O. Box 227, Mankato, Minnesota 56002
Creative Education and Creative Paperbacks are imprints
of The Creative Company
www.thecreativecompany.us

Design and production by Blue Design, Inc.
Art direction by Wyeth Morgan
Edited by Ana Brauer

Photographs by Getty Images/Florilegius, 6, Kriangkrai Thitimakorn, 28, Paddy Photography, 4–5, Punnawit Suwuttananun, 24; Unsplash/Fahrul Azmi, cover, 1, Fares Nimri, 21, Gautam Arora, 29, Hans-Jurgen Mager, 12, Himanshu Singh Gurjar, 27, katyayan gauniyal, 10, Rodrigo Rodrigues | WOLF Λ R T, 9, Rowan Heuvel, 3, 23, Sheraz Shaikh, 16, swastik chakraborty, 26; Wikimedia Commons/aiva., 14, Elliott & Fry, 17, Government of India/public domain, 8, 10, 14, 16, 20, 22, Original: AjoyDutta1997/Derivative work: Aristeas, CC BY-SA 4.0 , 18, public domain, 11

Library of Congress Cataloging-in-Publication Data
Names: Dittmer, Lori author
Title: India / by Lori Dittmer.
Description: Mankato, Minnesota : Creative Education and Creative Paperbacks, [2026] | Series: Spotlight on nations | Includes bibliographical references and index. | Audience: Ages 10-13 | Audience: Grades 4-6 | Summary: "Explore India's history, cultural diversity, family structures, festivals, landmarks, and technological advancements, plus its global influence and rich heritage. Written for middle-grade readers, this book includes timelines, sidebars, glossary, resources, and index"-- Provided by publisher.
Identifiers: LCCN 2025018194 (print) | LCCN 2025018195 (ebook) | ISBN 9798895810729 library binding | ISBN 9798896800255 paperback | ISBN 9798895811986 ebook
Subjects: LCSH: British--India--History | Technological innovations--Economic aspects--India | Information services industry--India--Juvenile literature | Families--India--Juvenile literature | Caste--India--History | Poverty--India | India--History | India--Civilization | India--Politics and government | India--Economic conditions | LCGFT: Literature
Classification: LCC DS407 .D57 2026 (print) | LCC DS407 (ebook) | DDC 954--dc23/eng/20250710
LC record available at https://lccn.loc.gov/2025018194
LC ebook record available at https://lccn.loc.gov/2025018195

Printed in the United States

CONTENTS

INTRODUCTION 4
Looking Back, Looking Ahead

CHAPTER 1: A RICH HISTORY 7
Mohandas Gandhi 8
Birth of Bangladesh 10

CHAPTER 2: THE REPUBLIC OF INDIA 13
Indian Space Research Organization (ISRO) 14
Harnessing the Sun 16

CHAPTER 3: FAMILY, SOCIETY, AND CELEBRATION 19
Caste System 20
Kumbh Mela 22

CHAPTER 4: THE COUNTRY OF BHARAT 25

All about India 29
Words to Know 30
Learn More 31
Index 32

INTRODUCTION

LOOKING BACK, LOOKING AHEAD

New Delhi sits along the Yamuna River in northern India. The city has been the capital of India for more than 100 years. But its history goes back much farther. New Delhi includes the remains of at least seven earlier cities. The first one was a fort. It was called Lal Kot, meaning "red fort," in 731 A.D. As new rulers conquered the area, they built near the city. Sometimes, they simply added onto it. Today, New Delhi is a sprawling center. It features **remnants** of more than 1,000 years of history. Monuments, palaces, and tombs are found throughout the area. But mixed with the old is new. New Delhi is also known for its growing technology industry. It is looking for ways to cut pollution and improve transportation. Like its capital city, India embraces its past as it looks to the future.

CLOSE-UP

Brahma

Brahma is an important god in Hinduism. He is called the Creator. He is part of a trio of gods with Vishnu and Shiva. Vishnu is the Preserver. Shiva is the Destroyer. Brahma's job is to create the universe and all living things.

CHAPTER ONE

A RICH HISTORY

The history of people living in India goes back thousands of years. The Indus civilization was one of the earliest known societies in the world. The people settled in the Indus River valley. This region is in northern India and Pakistan. The Indus people thrived for centuries. By about 1700 B.C., they were gone. Roughly 200 years later, another group moved to the area. These were Indo-Aryans. They came from central Asia. The Indo-Aryans used a language called Sanskrit. They wrote the Vedas. These texts described their history and rituals. The Vedas laid the foundation of the Hindu religion.

By the second century B.C., waves of people began to travel through the area. They followed the Silk Road. This network of routes connected Europe to Asia. People used it to trade goods. India was rich in spices and precious stones, such as diamonds. By 320 A.D., the Gupta dynasty controlled a large part of India. This dynasty made advancements in astronomy, art, and math. They developed the decimal system. They wrote a symbol for the concept of nothing—zero!

MILESTONES IN INDIA'S HISTORY

2600 BC

- The Indus civilization settles in the area that is today known as northern India and Pakistan

1500 BC

- The Indo-Aryan culture emerges and writes the Veda texts

In 1526, Babur arrived from Central Asia. He started the Mughal empire and became its first emperor. It was known for progress in government and architecture. The Mughal empire was a time of religious peace. By the 1600s, England had started the East India Company. It set up bases in India for trading goods. It built railroads to carry India's natural resources to England. Over time, the company gained more control in India. In 1858, The British took control from the Mughals, ending their empire. The British Raj, or rule, influenced India in many ways. It reformed the education system. It introduced English as a main language. But its rule also led to **famine** and poverty.

Indians banded together behind Mohandas Gandhi. He led them in nonviolent protest. In 1942, the Quit India Movement called for the British to leave India. Five years later, they did. India gained independence in 1947. It

CLOSE-UP

Traditional Yoga

Ancient people living in the Indus Valley developed and practiced yoga. Bronze seals from as long ago as 3000 B.C. show a figure performing yoga positions.

Mohandas Gandhi (1869–1948)

Mohandas Gandhi studied law in England before moving to South Africa. He worked there as a lawyer from 1893 to 1914. During this time, he experienced racial discrimination. In 1915, Gandhi returned to India to fight against injustice. He became a leader of the Indian National Congress and campaigned for India to be free from British rule. Gandhi led nonviolent protests. People began to call him "Mahatma," which means "great soul." His ideas later inspired civil rights leaders such as Martin Luther King, Jr. and Nelson Mandela.

876 AD

- The Chaturbhuj Temple is built in dedication to the Hindu god Vishnu. A plaque on the temple includes the earliest use of the o symbol for zero carved in stone

1526 AD

- The Mughal Empire begins, founded by Babur, a descendant of Mongolian warrior Genghis Khan

CLOSE-UP

Wildlife Wonders

Mudumalai National Park is in southwest India. Large groups of Bengal tigers and Asian elephants live there. Leopards, Indian bison, and wild dogs called dholes also roam through the park.

CHAPTER TWO

THE REPUBLIC OF INDIA

The government of the Republic of India has three parts. The executive branch includes a president and a prime minister. The president is elected to a five-year term. There is no term limit. The president serves as the head of state. The prime minister is the head of the Council of Ministers. The prime minister leads the government in India. The country also has a legislative branch. This includes two houses of parliament. The supreme court makes up the judicial branch. In 2022, Droupadi Murmu became president. Shri Narendra Modi was prime minister. India has eight union territories and 28 states. Union territories are led directly by the union government. Each state has its own elected government.

India's **economy** is one of the fastest growing in the world. It has a variety of natural resources. These include iron ore, diamonds, and petroleum. India's reserve of coal is the fourth largest in the world. The people of India

DECEMBER 31, 1600

England founds the East India Company to trade with areas including India, China, and Indonesia

1858

India comes under rule of the British crown. This period is known as the British Raj

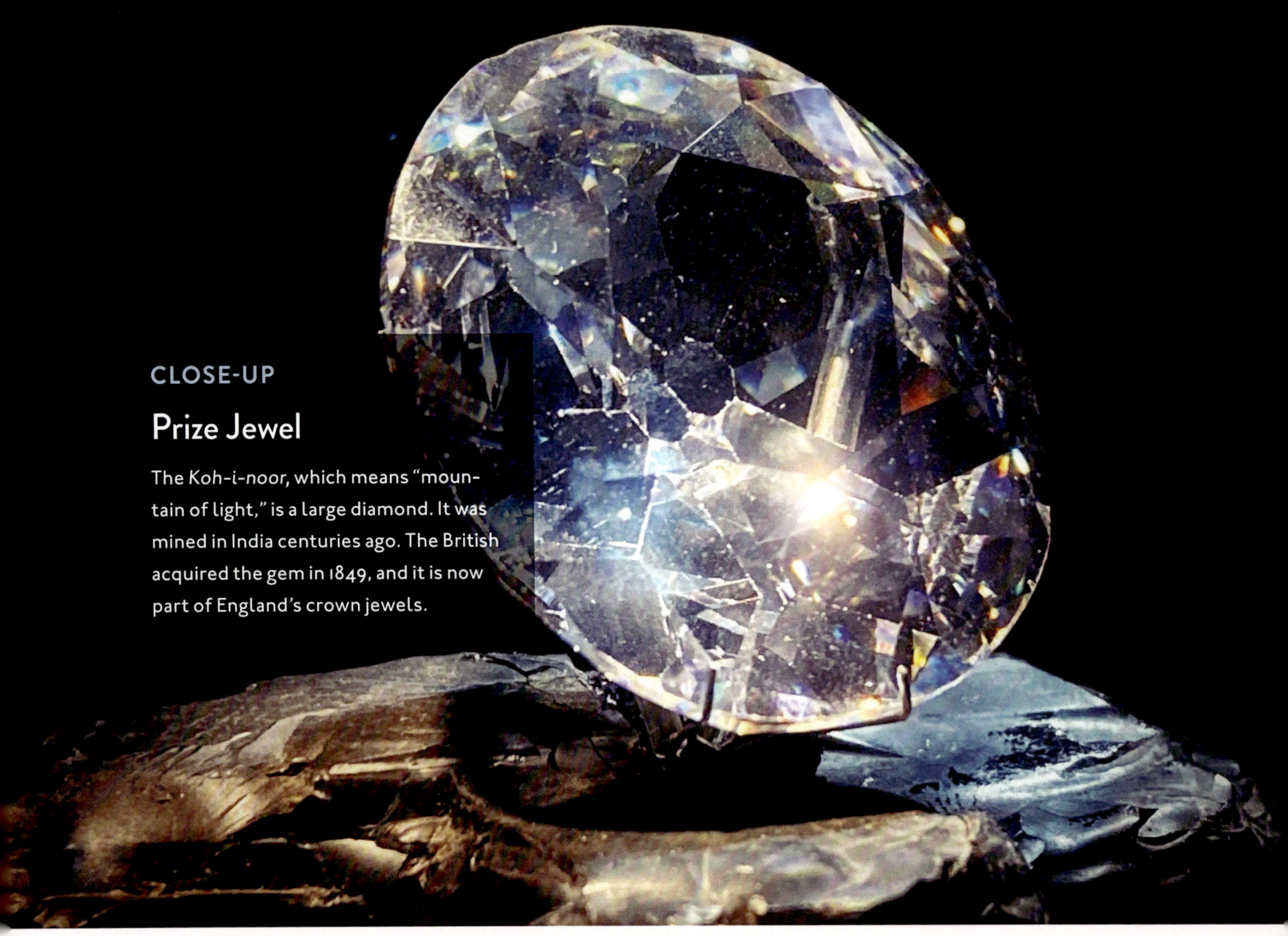

CLOSE-UP

Prize Jewel

The *Koh-i-noor*, which means "mountain of light," is a large diamond. It was mined in India centuries ago. The British acquired the gem in 1849, and it is now part of England's crown jewels.

Harnessing the Sun

India has more than 40 major solar power plants. The biggest is Bhadla Solar Park. Covering 14,000 acres (56 square kilometers), it is one of the largest in the world. Visible from space, Bhadla is nearly the size of the city of Manhattan, New York. Bhadla was built in the Thar Desert, near India's border with Pakistan. This area is hot and dry. The sun shines for about 300 days per year. It is difficult for people to live there. But it is a good site for millions of solar panels.

are some of the country's most important resources. India has a large pool of workers in science and technology. It is a global leader in information technology and software services. India has a growing space program. Over the last 10 years, India has created 4.7 million jobs in the space sector. The country has launched satellites to monitor weather patterns. These satellites help predict drought and flood conditions. This has helped the country's farmers and fishers.

India does not rely solely on its exports. A large portion of the economy is based on services used within the country. This makes the economy stable. It is less affected by the economies of other countries. India has focused on improving roads and buildings. During the last decade, it has doubled its number of airports. Several large solar fields produce energy. This will help the country meet its goal of reducing pollution.

In 2023, India passed China to become the most populated country in the world. It now has more than 1.4 billion people. The cities of Mumbai, Kolkata, and Delhi are some of the world's largest. As these cities grow, they have struggled to keep up with the people's needs. In some areas, there is not enough housing, so slums have formed. In slums, families often live in tiny, crowded shelters. India is working to reduce poverty by expanding access to education, jobs, and health care. Still, poverty is one of India's biggest challenges.

1876

Queen Victoria of England is named Empress of India

DECEMBER 2, 1911

British royals King George V (5) and Queen Mary land in Mumbai on their way to visit Delhi. A monument called the Gateway of India is completed in 1924 in honor of their visit

CLOSE-UP

Extensive Legal Framework

With 395 articles, 12 schedules, and more than 90 amendments, India's constitution is one of the longest and most detailed in the world.

HISTORICAL HIGHLIGHT

Indian Space Research Organization (ISRO)

India's space program put its first satellite, *Aryabhata*, into space in 1975. The Soviet program helped launch it. Since then, the ISRO has worked to grow its program. In 2023, India launched its own mission to the Moon. The *Chandryaan-3* landed near the Moon's south pole. The mission made India the first country to explore this region. As of 2025, India plans to send humans into space. If successful, it will be the fourth country to do so. India also plans to build its own space station by 2035.

1920

- Mahatma Gandhi begins the first civil disobedience campaign against the British Empire

AUGUST 15, 1947

- India gains independence from the British Empire. Jawaharlal Nehru becomes India's first prime minister

CLOSE-UP

Festival of Lights

Diwali is a festival celebrated in India to mark the victory of light over darkness and good over evil. People decorate the ground with colorful rangoli and light small candles called diyas to bring joy and good luck.

CHAPTER THREE

FAMILY, SOCIETY, AND CELEBRATION

India is incredibly diverse. Thousands of ethnic groups live within the country's borders. Hundreds of languages are spoken there. This gives the people of India a rich cultural **heritage**. Some of the most important parts of life involve family, society, religion, and festivals.

Family is central to life in India. Long ago, most marriages were planned by the parents of the bride and groom. The tradition goes back thousands of years. In ancient times, men from around the kingdom would compete in events. They fought to win the hand of a royal bride. Today, arranged marriages still happen, but not as often. In many families, the bride moves in with her husband's family. This might include his parents and other family members. The family's income goes into a common pool to benefit all members. The head of the family is the oldest male or female, and they make big decisions. Another important part of Indian life is caste, or social rank. People usually consider caste when choosing a spouse.

JANUARY 30, 1948

Mahatma Gandhi is assassinated on his way to an evening prayer meeting

JANUARY 1966

Nehru's daughter, Indira Gandhi, becomes India's first female prime minister

Celebrations are important in India. August 15 is India's Independence Day. It marks the end of British rule in 1947. People celebrate with parades and kite flying. Many other festivals are tied to religion. India is home to many religions. Four major ones began there: Hinduism, Buddhism, Sikhism, and Jainism. About 80 percent of Indians are Hindu. Hinduism includes many large celebrations. Holi is the festival of colors. It celebrates spring. People wear white clothes and throw colored powder on each other. Diwali is the festival of lights. It takes place over five days in October or November. During Diwali, people light lamps and give gifts. Every 12 years, the city of Prayagraj hosts the world's largest religious gathering. It is called the Maha Kumbh Mela. More than 400 million people attend.

Caste System

Society in India is divided into levels called *jati*, or castes. Originally, people were assigned a jati based on their occupation. Today, castes are passed down from one's parents. The caste system began centuries ago. The highest group is the Brahmin, who were priests. Next were warriors, merchants, and landowners. At the bottom were Sudra, who were peasants and servants. There are around 3,000 castes and 25,000 sub-castes, each linked to specific jobs. People who had dirty jobs, like cleaning streets, were called "untouchables" and were outside the caste system.

DECEMBER 16, 1971

- Pakistan splits into two countries, Pakistan and Bangladesh

APRIL 19, 1975

- With the help of the Soviet space program, the ISRO puts its first satellite, *Aryabhata*, into space

India has nearly 650,000 Hindu temples. Each one is dedicated to one of the many gods associated with the religion. In the Hindu faith, cows are sacred. Hindus do not eat beef. Cows appear in Hindu mythology alongside a variety of gods. Hindus believe cows should be protected. As a result, many cows are allowed to wander the streets.

CLOSE-UP

Taj Mahal

The Taj Mahal is one of the most famous buildings in the world. Mughal ruler Shah Jahan had it built during the 1600s. His wife, Mumtaz Mahal, died giving birth to their 14th child. Shah Jahan built the Taj Mahal for her tomb.

Dancing is an important part of festivals. There are eight classical dances in Hindu. Dancers tell stories of Hindu mythology. They speak through gestures and movement. Folk dances are popular in rural areas. Performers act out stories passed down from past generations.

Kumbh Mela

In Hindu mythology, the god Vishnu wrestled with demons. He took their golden pitcher. It held the nectar of **immortality**. The fight lasted 12 days. During that time, four drops of nectar fell to Earth. Each landed in a different city: Prayagraj, Haridwar, Ujjain, and Nashik. Today, the Pitcher Festival, or Kumbh Mela, takes place every three years. The event rotates among the four cities. The Great Pitcher Festival happens every 12 years. It is the world's largest religious gathering. Millions of people travel there to dip themselves in the waters of Triveni Sangam.

2023

India surpasses China to become the most populated country on Earth.

MAY 11, 2000

- Aastha Arora is born, tipping India's population to 1 billion

APRIL 2023

- India surpasses China to become the most populated country on Earth

CHAPTER FOUR

THE COUNTRY OF BHARAT

To the world, the country is known as India. Within its borders, people sometimes call it ***Bharat***. This name is from the Sanskrit language. India is the seventh-largest country in the world. Snow-covered Himalayan mountains sit along its north border. The Thar Desert stretches across northwestern India. India is a peninsula. The southern portion is surrounded by water—the Bay of Bengal, the Indian Ocean, and the Arabian Sea. From June through September, monsoon winds bring heavy rains. This time is known as the rainy season.

The people of India love movies. Bollywood is the center of India's film industry. It is based in Mumbai. Under British rule, the city was called Bombay. The film industry there began in the 1930s. The name Bollywood came from the combination of Bombay and Hollywood. Today, Bollywood is a booming business. It makes about 1,000 films each year. These movies are known for **choreographed** fight scenes and elaborate song and dance routines.

The influence of the British Empire remains today. The British introduced sports such as cricket, soccer, and golf. Kabaddi, however, is a

CLOSE-UP

Mighty Kanchenjunga

Kanchenjunga is the highest mountain in India. It stands 28,169 feet (8,586 meters) above sea level. In the world, only Mount Everest and K2 climb higher. People who live nearby believe a protector god lives at the top.

sport that began in India. It combines tag, wrestling, and chanting. The British also made tea popular across the country. Before they arrived, Indians drank herbal teas for their health. To feed their own love of tea, the British planted huge **plantations**. Because so many spices and tea leaves are grown in the country, tea is an inexpensive drink. On average, people in India drink three cups of tea each day.

The people of India deeply value their history. Both locals and visitors are drawn to the country's inspiring architecture of past cultures. The Taj Mahal is the most popular. It is known as one of the Seven New Wonders of the World. Made of white marble, its color changes from pink to white to gold, depending on the time of day. The Ellora Caves feature temples carved into rock, showcasing Buddhist, Hindu, and Jain monuments. The Gateway of India was built under British rule. It marks the spot where King George V (5) and Queen Mary landed in Mumbai in 1911.

After British rule ended, India changed the names of some of its cities. Bombay became Mumbai. Calcutta was changed to Kolkata. India's history is long and rich. From its earliest Indus civilization to the British Raj and into its independence today, India embraces its history. It will draw from this past to create a stronger future.

ALL ABOUT INDIA

Continent: Asia

Capital city: New Delhi

Population size: 1.43 billion

Main language spoken: Hindi, English

Type of government: Constitutional Republic

Currency: Indian rupee

Main religion practiced: Hindu

Colors on flag: Saffron (orange), white, and green, with a blue 24-spoked wheel in the white stripe

National flower: Lotus

WORDS to Know

choreograph to plan movements and steps to be performed in a dance

discrimination unjust treatment of different categories of people

economy how a nation produces goods and services and consumes them

famine an extreme shortage of food

heritage something that is passed down from one generation to the next

immortality the ability to live forever

plantation a large farm specializing in a single crop

remnant a small piece of something left behind from the original

LEARN MORE

Books

Bolte, Mari. *Taj Mahal*. Mankato, MN: Creative Eduation, Creative Paperbacks, 2025.

Green, Sara. *Ancient India*. Minneapolis, MN: Bellwether Publishing, 2020.

Van, R.L. *India*. Minneapolis: Big Buddy Books, an imprint of Abdo Publishing, 2023.

Websites

"Diwali: Festival of Lights." National Geographic Kids.

https://kids.nationalgeographic.com/pages/article/diwali

"India." Britannica Kids.

https://kids.britannica.com/kids/article/India/345707

"The Story of India." PBS.

https://www.pbs.org/thestoryofindia/

Documentaries

The Geography of India Explained

https://www.youtube.com/watch?vlsxBGIcdWtO4

Modern and Mystic (Full Episode) – India from Above – Nat Geo Wild

https://www.youtube.com/watch?vIQx-xTWQHI5c

Wonders of India – The Most Amazing Places in India – Travel Video 4K

https://www.youtube.com/watch?vIFM2OuVbkPVw

Note: Every effort has been made to ensure that any websites listed above were active at the time of publication. However, because of the nature of the Internet, it is impossible to guarantee that these sites will remain active indefinitely or that their contents will not be altered.

Visit

ELLORA CAVES

Explore temples from three religions—Buddhism, Hinduism, and Jainism—carved out of the rock in a series of caves.

Ellora Cave Road, Ellora, Aurangabad, Maharashtra 431005

GATEWAY OF INDIA

Visit the concrete arch, built during the British Raj, that overlooks the Mumbai harbor into the Arabian Sea.

Apollo Bandar, Colaba, Mumbai, Maharashtra 400001

HAWA MAHAL

View the five-story structure with 953 ornate windows, completed in 1799. It allowed royal women to watch scenes in the street without being seen.

Hawa Mahal Road, Badi Choupad, J.D.A. Market, Pink City, Jaipur, Rajasthan

TAJ MAHAL

Tour the iconic white marble mausoleum built in the 1600s for the wife of Mughal emperor Shah Jahan.

Tajganj, Agra, Uttar Pradesh 282001

INDEX

Babur, 8, 11
Bangladesh, 9, 10, 21
Bollywood, 25
British, 8, 13, 14, 15, 17, 20, 25, 26
castes, 19, 20
dancing, 22, 25
Diwali, 18, 20
empires, 8, 11, 17, 25
festivals, 18, 19, 20, 22
Gandhi, Mohandas, 8, 17, 19
government, 8, 13
Gupta dynasty, 7
Hindu, 6, 7, 9, 10, 11, 20, 22, 26
Indian Space Research Organization (ISRO), 15, 16, 21
Muslim, 9, 10
New Delhi, 4
Pakistan, 7, 9, 10, 14, 21
Taj Mahal, 22, 26
Thar Desert, 14, 25